MW00936766

LEADERSHIP

INSPIRATIONAL QUOTES
TO CREATE A WISE LEADER

TheQuoteWell

www.TheQuoteWell.com

Words are powerful! TheQuoteWell is committed to sharing inspiration and wisdom through the power of the written word. Visit our website for:

- ➤ **Free collections of quotes**
- ➤ **Free tweetable images of inspiration**
- ➤ **Articles about Love, Life, Leadership, and more!**

To:_____

From:_____

To Ricky Moura.
You have both the head and the heart of an enlightened leader.

Foreword

This book is the result of many hours of research. Thousands of quotes were evaluated based on their relevance to the title, their ability to inspire, and for the accuracy of their citations. Unfortunately, curating quotes is an imprecise science. Great words are often borrowed. In some cases, multiple attributions can be found. In other cases, no attribution can be given. There are also many quotes that reflect similar sentiments worded differently. In the end, it is the burden of the editor to determine which quotes are used and who receives credit. Any and all content decisions made in editing these quotes have been in service of the deeper purpose of this book; to provide humor, wisdom, and perspective to the reader.

-Julian P. Harvey, Contributing Editor

ords are powerful! They have the ability to touch the soul, change our lives, and even change the world around us.

This book is a treasure of insight on the subject of leadership, but there is more than one way to access its wealth. Many of these quotes have been derived through a lifetime of experience, and you may consider reading and contemplating only one at a time in order to appreciate their greater meaning. You may choose to read one first thing in the morning, then remain watchful for its relevance throughout your day, seeing how its wisdom can be applied in your own life. In this way, you will learn the profound truth contained in every quote through the lens of your personal experience.

You may also prefer to read through the entire book, perhaps seeking guidance on a specific challenge you are facing. As you do this, you will begin to hear a single voice that rises from the chorus of disparate personalities presented in this book. Many sentiments, though nuanced through the unique perspective and experiences of different people, convey common wisdom shared by all. These are the universal truths of leadership.

I invite you to consider how your life might evolve and how you might affect the lives of those around you by implementing these teachings on a personal level. Only by extending the lessons of this book beyond your workplace or organization into your home, relationships, and community will you discover that to become an enlightened leader is to be an enlightened person.

THE QUOTES

Martin Luther King, Jr. *(January 15th, 1929 - April 4th, 1968) was an American Baptist minister, activist, humanitarian, and leader in the African-American Civil Rights Movement. He advocated nonviolent civil disobedience as a means to advance the American Civil Rights Movement, until his assassination in 1968.*

A genuine leader is not a searcher for consensus but a molder of consensus. —Martin Luther King, Jr.

Believe in your ability to create the future. That's what leaders do. That is our job. Understand reality but never be imprisoned by it. Reality is a moment in time. The future has not yet been written. It is written by leaders. —Mark Miller

Good leaders make people feel that they're at the very heart of things, not at the periphery. Everyone feels that he or she makes a difference to the success of the organization. When that happens, people feel centered and that gives their work meaning.
—Warren G. Bennis

A great person attracts great people and knows how to hold them together. —Johann Wolfgang Von Goethe

What you cannot enforce, do not command. —Sophocles

The mediocre teacher tells. The good teacher explains. The superior teacher demonstrates. The great teacher inspires.
—William Arthur Ward

Keep your fears to yourself, but share your courage with others.
—Robert Louis Stevenson

Raymond A. "Ray" Kroc (October 5th, 1902 – January 14th, 1984) was a business visionary who built the most successful fast food company in the world.

The quality of a leader is reflected in the standards they set for themselves. —Ray Kroc

The function of leadership is to produce more leaders, not more followers. —Ralph Nader

To handle yourself, use your head. To handle others, use your heart. —Eleanor Roosevelt

Leaders think and talk about the solutions. Followers think and talk about the problems. —Brian Tracy

Leadership is a privilege to better the lives of others. It is not an opportunity to satisfy personal greed. —Mwai Kibaki

Whoever is under a man's power is under his protection too. —David J. Schwartz

If you seek honor and respect you will not find it, for a leader is powerless to elevate himself. It is only when you serve others without regard for self will honor, respect, and lasting success be found. —Stevenson Willis

Not the cry, but the flight of a wild duck, leads the flock to fly and follow. —Chinese proverb

If your actions inspire others to dream more, learn more, do more, and become more, you are a leader. —John Quincy Adams

Weigh whatever you are about to say. What will it do to your hearer; encouragement, edification, disappointment or fear? What will it do to your life; glorify, edify, beautify, or weigh you down? Speak well and things will go well. —Jaachynma N.E. Agu

People work harder, longer, and more creatively if they are motivated by the intrinsic pleasure of their work. Managers must do everything they can to make the value of jobs obvious and the joy in them accessible. —Robert Watson

Leadership is not so much about technique and methods as it is about opening the heart. Leadership is about inspiration of oneself and of others. Great leadership is about human experiences, not processes. Leadership is not a formula or a program. It is a human activity that comes from the heart and considers the hearts of others. It is an attitude, not a routine. —Lance Secretan

Samuel L. Clemens (November 30th, 1835 – April 21st, 1910), also known as Mark Twain, was an author, media personality, humorist, and shrewd social commentator during the late nineteenth century. His books and short stories are now regarded as classic American literature.

Keep away from people who try to belittle your ambitions. Small people always do that, but the really great make you feel that you too can become great. —Mark Twain

Do not follow where the path may lead. Go instead where there is no path, and leave a trail. —Ralph Waldo Emerson

A leader is one who knows the way, goes the way, and shows the way. —John C. Maxwell

Management is about arranging and telling. Leadership is about nurturing and enhancing. —Tom Peters

Leadership is a potent combination of strategy and character. But if you must be without one, be without the strategy.
—Norman Schwarzkopf

Emanuel James "Jim" Rohn (September 17th, 1930 – December 5th, 2009) was a motivational speaker and author on the subjects of happiness, success, and quality of life. His message has improved the lives of many.

A good objective of leadership is to help those who are doing poorly to do well, and to help those who are doing well to do even better. —Jim Rohn

If an incompetent chieftain is removed, seldom do we appoint his highest ranking subordinate to his place. —Attila the Hun

Leadership is solving problems. The day soldiers stop bringing you their problems is the day you have stopped leading them. They have either lost confidence that you can help or concluded you do not care. Either case is a failure of leadership. —Colin Powell

When you can't make them see the light, make them feel the heat. —Ronald Reagan

Good leadership consists of showing average people how to do the work of superior people. —John D. Rockefeller

No man will make a great leader who wants to do it all himself or get all the credit for doing it. —Andrew Carnegie

Outstanding leaders go out of their way to boost the self-esteem of their personnel. If people believe in themselves, it's amazing what they can accomplish. —Sam Walton

Leadership is practiced not so much in words as in attitude and in actions. —Harold S. Geneen

People buy into the leader before they buy into the vision.
—John C. Maxwell

Leadership is unlocking people's potential to become better.
—Bill Bradley

There are three secrets to managing. The first secret is have patience. The second is be patient. And the third most important secret is patience. —Chuck Tanner

Management is doing things right. Leadership is doing the right things. —Peter F. Drucker

Leadership is diving for a loose ball, getting the crowd involved, getting other players involved. It's being able to take it as well as dish it out. That's the only way you're going to get respect from the players. —Larry Bird

The more you become aware of and respond to the needs of others, the richer your own life becomes. —Mollie Marti

Leaders grasp nettles. —David Ogilvy

You're only as good as the people you hire. —Ray Kroc

A man who wants to lead the orchestra must turn his back on the crowd. —Max Lucado

Stephen R. Covey (October 24th, 1932– July 16th, 2012) was a university professor, businessman, renowned keynote speaker, and author of several hugely popular books on the subjects of personal success and growth. His works are considered by many to be modern classics on the subject of success and self-improvement.

Management is efficiency in climbing the ladder of success. Leadership determines whether the ladder is leaning against the right wall. —Stephen Covey

Men make history and not the other way around. In periods where there is no leadership, society stands still. Progress occurs when courageous, skillful leaders seize the opportunity to change things for the better. —Harry S. Truman

Leadership is a matter of having people look at you and gain confidence, seeing how you react. If you're in control, they're in control. —Tom Landry

The secret to success is good leadership, and good leadership is all about making the lives of your team members or workers better. —Tony Dungy

One of the tests of leadership is the ability to recognize a problem before it becomes an emergency. —Arnold H. Glasow

Our chief want is someone who will inspire us to be what we know we could be. —Ralph Waldo Emerson

Truly powerful people have great humility. They do not try to impress, they do not try to be influential. They simply are. People are magnetically drawn to them. They are most often very silent and focused, aware of their core selves. They never persuade, nor do they use manipulation or aggressiveness to get their way. They listen. If there is anything they can offer to assist you, they offer it. If not, they are silent. —Sanaya Roman

A leader is like a shepherd. He stays behind the flock, letting the most nimble go out ahead, whereupon the others follow, not realizing that all along they are being directed from behind. —Nelson Mandela

Leaders are not, as we are often led to think, people who go along with huge crowds following them. Leaders are people who go their own way without caring, or even looking to see, whether anyone is following them. 'Leadership qualities' are not the qualities that enable people to attract followers, but those that enable them to do without them. They include, at the very least, courage, endurance, patience, humor, flexibility, resourcefulness, stubbornness, a keen sense of reality, and the ability to keep a cool and clear head, even when things are going badly. True leaders, in short, do not make people into followers, but into other leaders. —John Holt

The greatest leader is not necessarily the one who does the greatest things. He is the one that gets the people to do the greatest things. —Ronald Reagan

I cannot trust a man to control others who cannot control himself. —Robert E. Lee

A leader takes people where they want to go. A great leader takes people where they don't necessarily want to go, but ought to be. —Rosalynn Carter

Leaders must be close enough to relate to others, but far enough ahead to motivate them. —John C. Maxwell

If you want to build a ship, don't drum up the men to gather wood, divide the work, and give orders. Instead, teach them to yearn for the vast and endless sea. —Antoine de Saint-Exupéry

The key to successful leadership is influence, not authority.
—Kenneth H. Blanchard

Too many leaders value their popularity, protecting it at all cost, degrading their credibility. —Noel DeJesus

I cannot give you a formula for success, but I can give you the formula for failure; try to please everybody.
—Herbert Bayard Swope

A leader must lead. Where others see obstacles, he must see opportunities. When others see problems, he must see possibilities. Civilization is not built on a negation but on an affirmation, an affirmation of the bright and promising possibilities that the future holds for those who are enterprising enough to pursue them. —David J. Vaughan

Rank does not confer privilege or give power. It imposes responsibility. —Peter F. Drucker

The challenge of leadership is to be strong but not rude, be kind but not weak, be bold but not a bully, be humble but not timid, be proud but not arrogant, have humour but without folly.
—Jim Rohn

A true dreamer is one who knows how to navigate in the dark.
—John Paul Warren

Average leaders raise the bar on themselves. Good leaders raise the bar for others. Great leaders inspire others to raise their own bar. —Orrin Woodward

When you accept a leadership role, you take on extra responsibility for your actions toward others. —Kelley Armstrong

"Give as few orders as possible", his father had told him once long ago. "Once you've given orders on a subject, you must always give orders on that subject." —Frank Herbert

The first key to leadership is self-control. —Jack Weatherford

Accountants are in the past, managers are in the present, and leaders are in the future. —Paul Orfalea

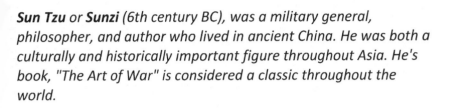

Sun Tzu or Sunzi (6th century BC), was a military general, philosopher, and author who lived in ancient China. He was both a culturally and historically important figure throughout Asia. He's book, "The Art of War" is considered a classic throughout the world.

Regard your soldiers as your children and they will follow you into the deepest valleys. Look upon them as your own beloved sons, and they will stand by you even unto death. —Sun Tzu

There go the people. I must follow them for I am their leader. —Alexandre Ledru-Rollin

Managers maintain an efficient status quo while leaders attack the status quo to create something new. —Orrin Woodward

True greatness, true leadership, is achieved not by reducing men to one's service but in giving oneself in selfless service to them. —J. Oswald Sanders

You cease to be a leader when you manipulate with your ego instead of convincing by your inspiration. —Israelmore Ayivor

The world is full of stupid people. That's why we have rules. But with enough intelligence, a person can be above the rules. She can make rules. —Daniel Nayeri

The power to lead is the power to mislead, and the power to mislead is the power to destroy. —Thomas S. Monson

The best executive is the one who has sense enough to pick good men to do what he wants done, and self-restraint to keep from meddling with them while they do it. —Theodore Roosevelt

"The first key to leadership was self-control, particularly the mastery of pride, which was something more difficult to subdue than a wild lion and anger, which was more difficult to defeat than the greatest wrestler." He warned them that, "If you can't swallow your pride, you can't lead."
—Jack Weatherford

It's not about you. It's about them. —Clint Eastwood

Leaders are people who believe so passionately that they can seduce other people into sharing their dream. —Warren G. Bennis

The condition of leadership adds new degrees of solitariness to the basic solitude of mankind. Every order that we issue increases the extent to which we are alone, and every show of deference which is extended to us separates us from our fellows.
—Thornton Wilder

Successful leaders see the opportunities in every difficulty rather than the difficulty in every opportunity. —Reed Markham

Our expectation in ourselves must be higher than our expectation in others. —Victor Manuel Rivera

Seth Godin (born July 10, 1960) is an American author, public speaker, entrepreneur and marketing professional. He is known for his innovative perspective on the subject of emerging paradigms within the fields of business and marketing.

The secret of leadership is simple: Do what you believe in. Paint a picture of the future. Go there. People will follow. —Seth Godin

The only real training for leadership is leadership. —Antony Jay

The manager asks how and when. The leader asks what and why.
—Warren G. Bennis

You have to lift a person up before you can really put them in their place. —Criss Jami

A leader without a clear vision and plans only abuses his power because visions, dreams and plans are the fulcrum along which the loads of success will spine by your own efforts. And where power is abused, there is manipulation instead of inspiration.
—Israelmore Ayivor

Asking questions will get you the performance you are after far more than dictating demands. —Dan James

One of the fundamental aspects of leadership, I realized more and more, is the ability to instill confidence in others when you yourself are feeling insecure. —Howard Schultz

A leader should demonstrate his thoughts and opinions through his actions, not through his words. —Jack Weatherford

A confident leader is like a duck. Above the water he is calm and poised, while below the water he is driven by a flurry of focused activity. —Todd Stocker

If you fail to offer yourself for leadership then accept the blind man who is leading you. —Fenley Douglas

When you don't see nothing wrong in anything you do, then you are doing everything wrong. —Richmond Akhigbe

Leadership is communicating to people their worth and potential so clearly that they are inspired to see it in themselves.
—L. David Marquet

Your vehicle of leadership is fueled by your willingness to learn. You can't lead if you can't learn! —Israelmore Ayivor

I believe leaders should be a questioning machine, rather than an answering machine. —Saji Ijiyemi

Leadership is about embedding the right mindset into the organizational culture to ensure execution excellence.
—Author unknown

Great leadership involves three things; the ability to realize when you are wrong, a willingness to learn from it, and an eagerness to change course if necessary. —Jeffrey Fry

One of the greatest skills and gifts is to focus on a person. Make them feel as though they're the only person in the world.
—Rhonda Rhyne

When you empower your people, your business will grow.
—Ifeanyi Enoch Onuoha

The first responsibility of a leader is to define reality. The last is to say thank you. In between, the leader is a servant. —Max DePree

Lead, follow, or get out of the way. —Thomas Paine

There are few second chances when it comes to establishing your leadership legacy. —Scott H. Dearduff

Leaders exude courage by sacrificing their popularity for their values and beliefs. —Noel DeJesus

When faced with a challenging or difficult situation, the best leaders most often respond with courage. Less mature leaders or non-leaders often choose another path, a path with less risk, less conflict, and less personal discomfort. —Mark Miller

Leadership is an action, not a position. —Donald McGannon

A ruler should be slow to punish and swift to reward. —Ovid

When leaders reframe customers into guests, and results into experiences, profits escalate. —Eric Schiffer

All organizations are perfectly designed to get the results they are now getting. If we want different results, we must change the way we do things. —Tom Northup

The leader has to be practical and a realist, yet must talk the language of the visionary and the idealist. —Eric Hoffer

True leadership lies in guiding others to success, in ensuring that everyone is performing at their best, doing the work they are pledged to do and doing it well. —Bill Owens

Warren G. Bennis (born March 8, 1925) is a scholar, speaker, and author on the subject of leadership. His work is foundational to the field of leadership research studies, which he is widely credited with creating.

The most dangerous leadership myth is that leaders are born, that there is a genetic factor to leadership. That's nonsense. In fact, the opposite is true. Leaders are made rather than born.
—Warren G. Bennis

Leadership is getting people to work for you when they are not obligated. —Fred Smith

The price of greatness is responsibility. —Winston Churchill

There's plenty of room at the top, but there's no room to sit down. —Helen Downey

Too many companies believe people are interchangeable. Truly gifted people never are. They have unique talents. Such people cannot be forced into roles they are not suited for, nor should they be. Effective leaders allow great people to do the work they were born to do. —Warren G. Bennis

How was your day? If your answer was 'fine', then I don't think you were leading. —Seth Godin

No true leader burdened his followers with a greater load than they could carry, and no true leader sets too fast a pace for his follows to keep up. —Malcolm X

The way I would measure leadership is this: of the people that are working with me, how many wake up in the morning thinking that the company is theirs? —David M. Kelley

You manage things; you lead people.
—Rear Admiral Grace Murray Hopper

You cannot climb up to a true leadership position unless you use the ladder of integrity. —Israelmore Ayivor

Before you are a leader, success is all about growing yourself. When you become a leader, success is all about growing others. —Jack Welch

A leader is a dealer in hope. —Napoleon Bonaparte

Leadership begins by asking how you can make things better. —Jeffrey Fry

He who has never learned to obey cannot be a good commander. —Aristotle

Become the kind of leader that people would follow voluntarily; even if you had no title or position. —Brian Tracy

Outstanding leaders go out of their way to boost the self-esteem of their personnel. If people believe in themselves, it's amazing what they can accomplish. —Sam Walton

A true leader has the confidence to stand alone, the courage to make tough decisions, and the compassion to listen to the needs of others. He does not set out to be a leader, but becomes one by the equality of his actions and the integrity of his intent. —Douglas MacArthur

Colin Luther Powell (born April 5, 1937) is a retired four-star United States Army general, former U.S. Secretary of State, former Chairman of the Joint Chiefs of Staff, and former Commander of the U.S. Army in Iraq.

Great leaders are almost always great simplifiers, who can cut through argument, debate, and doubt, to offer a solution everybody can understand. —General Colin Powell

Before we acquire great power we must acquire wisdom to use it well. —Ralph Waldo Emerson

Where there is no vision, the people perish. —Proverbs 29:18

You don't lead by pointing and telling people some place to go. You lead by going to that place and making a case. —Ken Kesey

What you do has far greater impact than what you say.
—Stephen Covey

Remember the difference between a boss and a leader; a boss says, "Go!" A leader says, "Let's go!" —E.M. Kelly

A chief is a man who assumes responsibility. He says, "I was beaten." He does not say, "My men were beaten."
—Antoine de Saint-Exupery

Nothing so conclusively proves a man's ability to lead others as what he does from day to day to lead himself.—Thomas J. Watson

Leadership is not magnetic personality. That can just as well be a glib tongue. It is not making friends and influencing people. That is flattery. Leadership is lifting a person's vision to higher sights, the raising of a person's performance to a higher standard, the building of a personality beyond its normal limitations.
—Peter F. Drucker

Leadership is the ability to establish standards and manage a creative climate where people are self-motivated toward the mastery of long-term constructive goals, in a participatory environment of mutual respect, compatible with personal values.
—Mike Vance

It is not this way among you, but whoever wishes to become great among you, shall be your servant, and whoever wishes to be first among you shall be your slave. —Jesus Christ

When I give a minister an order, I leave it to him to find the means to carry it out. —Napoleon Bonaparte

The supreme quality for leadership is unquestionably integrity. Without it, no real success is possible no matter whether it is on a section gang, a football field, in an army, or in an office. —Dwight D. Eisenhower

Let him who would be moved to convince others, be first moved to convince himself. —Thomas Carlyle

Albert Einstein (March 14th, 1879 - April 18th, 1955) was one of the most brilliant scientific minds in history. His revolutionary theories changed human understanding of time, space, matter, and energy.

Setting an example is not the main means of influencing others. It is the only means. —Albert Einstein

A statesman gains little by the arbitrary exercise of ironclad authority upon all occasions that offer, for this wounds the just pride of his subordinates and thus tends to undermine his strength. A little concession now and then where it can do no harm is the wiser policy. —Mark Twain

Not everybody can be famous but everybody can be great because greatness is determined by service. You only need a heart full of grace and a soul generated by love.
—Martin Luther King, Jr.

The leaders who work most effectively, it seems to me, never say "I." And that's not because they have trained themselves not to say "I". They don't *think* "I." They think "we." They think "team." They understand their job to be to make the team function. They accept responsibility and don't sidestep it, but "we" get the credit. This is what creates trust, what enables you to get the task done.
—Peter F. Drucker

When the sea was calm, all ships alike showed mastership in floating. —William Shakespeare

A great leader's courage to fulfill his vision comes from passion, not position. —John Maxwell

The task of the leader is to get his people from where they are to where they have not been. —Henry Kissinger

Leadership is based on a spiritual quality; the power to inspire, the power to inspire others to follow. —Vince Lombardi

Leaders should strive for authenticity over perfection.
—Sheryl Sandberg

Leadership is about taking responsibility, not making excuses.
—Mitt Romney

Genuine leadership comes from the quality of your vision and your ability to spark others to extraordinary performance.
—Jack Welch

Leadership is the capacity to translate vision into reality.
—Warren G. Bennis

To be a great leader, and so always master of the situation, one must of necessity have been a great thinker in action. An eagle was never yet hatched from a goose's egg. —James Thomas

To do great things is difficult, but to command great things is more difficult. —Friedrich Nietzsche

Henry Ford (July 30th, 1863 – April 7th, 1947) was an American inventor, entrepreneur, and industrialist of the twentieth century. His invention of assembly line mass production transformed the manufacturing industry, and thus the world around us.

Don't find fault, find a remedy. —Henry Ford

The power is detested, and miserable the life of him who wishes to be feared rather than to be loved.—Cornelius Nepos

The leader's job is not to cover all the bases. It is to see that all bases are covered. —James Crupi

Effective leadership is not about making speeches or being liked. Leadership is defined by results not attributes.—Peter F. Drucker

Only packs of jackals have dynastic succession. Whereas prides of lions have a fight between rival lions for leadership.
—Author unknown

Be the chief but never the lord. —Lao Tzu

Leadership is defined by results, not by attributes.
—Peter F. Drucker

Don't follow the crowd. Let the crowd follow you.
—Margaret Thatcher

Leadership is the art of getting someone else to do something you want done because he wants to do it. —Dwight D. Eisenhower

Don't tell people how to do things. Tell them what to do and let them surprise you with their results. —George S. Patton Jr.

Leadership is not about titles, positions or flowcharts. It is about one life influencing another. —John C. Maxwell

It's hard to lead a cavalry charge if you think you look funny on a horse. —Adlai Stevenson

A leader who doesn't hesitate before he sends his nation into battle is not fit to be a leader. —Golda Meir

We live in a society obsessed with public opinion, but leadership has never been about popularity. —Marco Rubio

A great leader creates more great leaders, and does not reduce the institution to a single person.
—Sheikh Mohammed bin Rashid Al Maktoum

Leadership is getting someone to do what they don't want to do, to achieve what they want to achieve. —Tom Landry

95% of success in business lies in our ability to read, lead and influence the behaviors of ourselves and others.
—Daniel Goldman

Leadership is doing what is right when no one is watching.
—George Van Valkenburg

Winners get to the top and turn around to see those they have defeated. Leaders get to the top and turn around to help others achieve the same. —Dan Churches

A leader has the vision and conviction that a dream can be achieved. He inspires the power and energy to get it done.
—Ralph Lauren

The task of leadership is not to put greatness into people, but to elicit it, for the greatness is there already. —John Buchan

Leaders are more powerful role models when they learn than when they teach. —Rosabeth Moss Kantor

The sky cannot have two suns. —Chiang Kai-Shek

The leader who exercises power with honor will work from the inside out, starting with himself. —Blaine Lee

To command is to serve, nothing more and nothing less. —Andre Malraux

Leadership is the key to 99 percent of all successful efforts. —Erskine Bowles

John C. Maxwell *(born 1947) is a prolific American author and international keynote speaker on the subject of leadership.*

Tend to the people and they will tend to the business.
—John C. Maxwell

The only safe ship in a storm is leadership. —Faye Wattleton

A leader leads by example, whether he intends to or not.
—John Quincy Adams

A community is like a ship. Everyone ought to be prepared to take the helm. —Henrik Ibsen

A real leader faces the music, even when he doesn't like the tune.
—Author unknown

A good leader inspires people to have confidence in the leader. A great leader inspires people to have confidence in themselves. —Eleanor Roosevelt

Leadership cannot really be taught. It can only be learned. —Harold Geneen

Leadership is the special quality which enables people to stand up and pull the rest of us over the horizon. —James Fisher

Leadership should be more participative than directive, more enabling than performing. —Mary D. Poole

Leadership should be born out of the understanding of the needs of those who would be affected by it. —Marian Anderson

A sense of humor is part of the art of leadership, of getting along with people, of getting things done. —Dwight D. Eisenhower

Leaders are designers, stewards, and teachers. They are responsible for building organizations where people continually expand their abilities to understanding complexity, clarify vision, and improve shared mental models, that is, they are responsible for learning. —Peter Senge

Presidents, leaders, to be effective have to represent the whole to the parts and to the world outside. They may live in the centre but they must not be the centre. To reinforce the common sense they must be a constant teacher, ever travelling, ever talking, ever listening, the chief missionary of the common cause.
—Charles Handy

The best leaders are the best note takers, best askers and best learners. They are shameless thieves. —Tom Peters

If you talk to a man in a language he understands, that goes to his head. If you talk to him in his language, that goes to his heart. —Nelson Mandela

Kind words can be short and easy to speak, but their echoes are truly endless. —Mother Theresa

The only test of leadership is that somebody follows. —Robert K. Greenleaf

It is important that an aim never be defined in terms of activity or methods. It must always relate directly to how life is better for everyone. The aim of the system must be clear to everyone in the system. The aim must include plans for the future. The aim is a value judgment. —W. Edwards Deming

I believe in businesses where you engage in creative thinking, and where you form some of your deepest relationships. If it isn't about the production of the human spirit, we are in big trouble. —Anita Roddick

It is not fair to ask of others what you are not willing to do yourself. —Eleanor Roosevelt

*Lao Tzu also called **Lao Zi, Lao Tzu, Lao Tse, or Lao Tze** (c. 6th-5th century BCE) was a philosopher and poet of ancient China. He is credited with composing the "Tao Te Ching", a philosophical and spiritual work widely regarded as a masterpiece.*

To lead people, walk beside them. As for the best leaders, the people do not notice their existence. The next best, the people honor and praise. The next, the people fear. And the next, the people hate. When the best leader's work is done, the people say, "We did it ourselves!" —Lao Tzu

You can build a throne with bayonets, but you can't sit on it for long. —Boris Yeltsin

A councilor ought not to sleep the whole night through, a man to whom the populace is entrusted, and who has many responsibilities. —Homer

A leader does not deserve the name unless he is willing occasionally to stand alone. —Henry Kissinger

A leader is someone who helps improve the lives of other people or improve the system they live under. —Sam Houston

A leader must have the courage to act against an expert's advice.
—James Callaghan

A leader who confines his role to his people's experience dooms himself to stagnation; a leader who outstrips his people's experience runs the risk of not being understood.
—Henry Kissinger

Always drink upstream from the herd. —Will Rogers

It is a well-known fact that those people who must want to rule people are, ipso facto, those least suited to do it. Anyone who is capable of getting themselves made President should on no account be allowed to do the job. —Douglas Adams

It is the nature and the advantage of strong people that they can bring out the crucial questions and form a clear opinion about them. The weak always have to decide between alternatives that are not their own. —Dietrich Bonhoeffer

Ten soldiers wisely led will beat a hundred without a head. —Euripides

The genius of a good leader is to leave behind him a situation which common sense, without the grace of genius, can deal with successfully. —Walter Lippmann.

The great leaders are like the best conductors. They reach beyond the notes to reach the magic in the players. —Blaine Lee

We must be part of the general staff at the inception, rather than the ambulance drivers at the bitter end. —Lane Kirkland

When you're leading, don't talk. —Thomas E. Dewey

People will not follow a leader with moral incongruities for long. Every time you compromise character you compromise leadership. The foundation of firm leadership is character. —Bill Hybels

Once a leader delegates, he should show utmost confidence in the people he has entrusted. —A.B. Simpson

The ultimate measure of a man is not where he stands in moments of comfort and convenience, but where he stands at times of challenge and controversy. —Martin Luther King, Jr.

Courage is what it takes to stand up and speak. Courage is also what it takes to sit down and listen. —Winston Churchill

A bold onset is half the battle. —Giuseppe Garibaldi

Absolute identity with one's cause is the first and great condition of successful leadership. —Woodrow Wilson

A competent leader can get efficient service from poor troops, while on the contrary, an incapable leader can demoralize the best of troops. —John J. Pershing

A first rate organizer is never in a hurry. He is never late. He always keeps up his sleeve a margin for the unexpected —Arnold Bennett

A good general not only sees the way to victory, he also knows when victory is impossible. —Polybius

A great man is one who can have power and not abuse it.
—Henry L. Doherty

A leader's role is to raise people's aspirations for what they can become and to release their energies so they will try to get there.
—David R. Gergen

All of the great leaders have had one characteristic in common. It was the willingness to confront unequivocally the major anxiety of their people in their time. This, and not much else, is the essence of leadership. —John Kenneth Galbraith

Character matters. Leadership descends from character. —Rush Limbaugh

The growth and development of people is the highest calling of leadership. —Harvey Firestone

Peter F. Drucker (November 19th, 1909 – November 11, 2005) was a business management consultant, educator, author, and speaker. His innovative ideas helped define modern corporate management philosophy.

Charisma becomes the undoing of leaders. It makes them inflexible, convinced of their own infallibility, unable to change.
—Peter F. Drucker

The leadership instinct you are born with is the backbone. You develop the funny bone and the wishbone that go with it.
—Elaine Agather

Most important, leaders can conceive and articulate goals that lift people out of their petty preoccupations and unite them in pursuit of objectives worthy of their best efforts. —John Gardner

Dictators ride to and fro upon tigers which they dare not dismount. And the tigers are getting hungry. —Winston Churchill

Don't necessarily avoid sharp edges. Occasionally they are necessary to leadership. —Donald Rumsfeld

Earn your leadership every day. —Michael Jordan

Education is the mother of leadership. —Wendell Willkie

Effective leadership is putting first things first. Effective management is discipline, carrying it out. —Stephen Covey

Following the herd often leads to the slaughterhouse.
—Nerella Campigotto

Forget about yourself and just think of your people. It's always the people who make things happen. —Corazon Aquino

Good leaders must first become good servants.
—Robert Greenleaf

He who has great power should use it lightly. —Seneca

High sentiments always win in the end. The leaders who offer blood, toil, tears, and sweat always get more out of their followers than those who offer safety and a good time. When it comes to the pinch, human beings are heroic. —George Orwell

Humans are ambitious and rational and proud. And we don't fall in line with people who don't respect us and who we don't believe have our best interests at heart. We are willing to follow leaders, but only to the extent that we believe they call on our best, not our worst. —Rachel Maddow

If a rhinoceros were to enter this restaurant now, there is no denying he would have great power here. But I should be the first to rise and assure him that he had no authority whatever.
—G.K. Chesterton

I forgot to shake hands and be friendly. It was an important lesson about leadership. —Lee Iacocca

If the blind lead the blind, both shall fall in the ditch.
—Jesus Christ

Mohandas K. Gandhi (October 2nd, 1869 - January 30th, 1948) Espousing peaceful, non-violent resistance, Gandhi led the nation of India in the overthrow of British imperial rule during the early twentieth century. His methods inspired rights movements throughout history and around the world. To this day he is considered one of the greatest spiritual leaders who ever lived.

I suppose leadership at one time meant muscles, but today it means getting along with people. —Mahatma Gandhi

I think leadership comes from integrity, that you do whatever you ask others to do. I think there are non-obvious ways to lead. Just by providing a good example as a parent, a friend, a neighbor, makes it possible for other people to see better ways to do things. Leadership does not need to be a dramatic 'fist in the air' and 'trumpets blaring' activity. —Scott Berkun

Ill can he rule the great that cannot reach the small.
—Edmund Spenser

Innovation distinguishes between a leader and a follower.
—Steve Jobs

It is better to lead from behind and to put others in front,
especially when you celebrate victory when nice things occur. You
take the front line when there is danger. Then people will
appreciate your leadership. —Nelson Mandela

It is better to have a lion at the head of an army of sheep, than a sheep at the head of an army of lions. —Daniel Defoe

It is impossible to imagine anything which better becomes a ruler than mercy. —Seneca

I used to think that running an organization was equivalent to conducting a symphony orchestra. But I don't think that's quite it. It's more like jazz. There is more improvisation.
—Warren G. Bennis

Lead and inspire people. Don't try to manage and manipulate people. Inventories can be managed but people must be lead.
—Ross Perot

Leaders are simultaneously champions of the vision, custodians of the values, and shepherds of the people. —Manie Bosman

No institution can possibly survive if it needs geniuses or supermen to manage it. It must be organized in such a way as to be able to get along under a leadership composed of average human beings. —Peter F. Drucker

Leadership cannot just go along to get along. Leadership must meet the moral challenge of the day. —Jesse Jackson

Leadership is getting players to believe in you. If you tell a teammate you're ready to play as tough as you're able to, you'd better go out there and do it. Players will see right through a phony. And they can tell when you're not giving it all you've got. —Larry Bird

Leadership is mostly about the courage and willingness to do what it takes and sacrifice what is needed to achieve what is required. —Manie Bosman

Leadership is understanding people and involving them to help you do a job. That takes all of the good characteristics, like integrity, dedication of purpose, selflessness, knowledge, skill, implacability, as well as determination not to accept failure. —Admiral Arleigh A. Burke

Management means, in the last analysis, the substitution of thought for brawn and muscle, of knowledge for folklore and superstition, and of cooperation for force. —Peter F. Drucker

Misfortunes, untoward events, lay open, disclose the skill of a general, while success conceals his weakness, his weak points. —Horace

Israelmore Ayivor (December 16, 1989) *Educated in Ghana, Israelmore Ayivor is a profound and prolific speaker, author, and life coach on the subjects of self-improvement, leadership and personal development.*

If the problems you have this year are the same problems you had last year, then you are not a leader. Rather, you are a problem on your own that must be solved. —Israelmore Ayivor

My own definition of leadership is this: The capacity and the will to rally men and women to a common purpose and the character which inspires confidence. — General Bernard Montgomery

Nearly all men can stand adversity, but if you want to test a man's character, give him power. —Abraham Lincoln

Next to the assumption of power is the responsibility of relinquishing it. —Benjamin Disraeli

No general can fight his battles alone. He must depend upon his lieutenants, and his success depends upon his ability to select the right man for the right place. —Philip Armour

Leadership can be thought of as a capacity to define oneself to others in a way that clarifies and expands a vision of the future. —Edwin H. Friedman

No man is good enough to govern another man without that other's consent. —Abraham Lincoln

People are more easily led than driven. —David Harold Fink

Praise works with only three types of people: men, women, and children. —Author unknown

So much of what we call management consists in making it difficult for people to work. —Peter F. Drucker

The art of leadership is saying no, not saying yes. It is very easy to say yes. —Tony Blair

The greatest good you can do for another is not just share your riches but to reveal to them their own. —Benjamin Disraeli

The real leader has no need to lead. He is content to point the way. —Henry Miller

There are three essentials to leadership: humility, clarity and courage. —Fuchan Yuan

Acknowledgments

This book would not have been possible without the efforts of a hardworking team of researchers. Their discriminating sensibilities have made this a significant collection of wisdom.

About TheQuoteWell

Words are powerful! And no words are more powerful than inspirational quotes. TheQuoteWell is passionate about spreading hope, joy, wisdom, and humor through the power of the written word. Follow us on Twitter, Facebook, YouTube, and Google+ for access to FREE wisdom daily.

TheQuoteWell books are curated collections. Each book is the result of careful selection for only the best quotes from past through present on the subjects of Love, Life, Leadership, and more! The result is a chorus of profound wisdom emanating from a fascinating diversity of speakers. If you enjoyed this volume, visit our website for other titles.

If you enjoyed this book and think others might also, PLEASE leave a five star review on Amazon!

Check out other titles from TheQuoteWell.
Available in paperback and all digital formats.

Words. Change. Lives.
Who do you want to Inspire?

Made in the USA
Coppell, TX
11 April 2020